SHHHH! IT'S A SECRET

HOW TO

COMPETE

AGAINST WALMART AND THE INTERNET

Business Survival Tips for the 21st Century

F. E. Tabor

What this book isn't:

Basic money management; go to your accountant.
Get rich quick; don't believe in it.
Complete; learning never ends.

Who this book is for:

The American government defines "small business" as any with fewer than 500 employees. We with fewer than thirty are almost invisible, but together our *very* small businesses employ over 65% of all Americans. If you are one of the millions who own a small business,

This book is for you.

What this book is:

Fifteen private conversations from one Small Business Owner (me), to you. Plus a few ideas to help us all stay in the profit groove—no matter how much the news tries to turn us into quitters!

Who am I to Offer Advice?

I am a forty year small business survivor. I started as a self-employed job-owner, eventually needed paid co-workers (employees). I evolved to business owner with over two dozen employees doing over $1,500,000.00 annually. Then embezzlements, cancer, a recession, all hit at once. I plummeted to two-thirds the income and only seven employees.

My road has been bumpy, full of mistakes and always entertaining!

May what I am about to share help make your business ride smoother.

Copyright 2012 Fran Tabor

Cover image courtesy of Milo827 | Dreamstime.com
Cover by Terry Compton

This is dedicated to my parents, who taught me what others call failure is really an educational experience.

The greater the education, the more expensive it usually is.
My father told me many times, it is entirely up to me to get my money's worth out of life's lessons.

Thank you, Mom and Dad.
My only regret is not learning as fast as both of you taught!

Table of Contents

1. Fletchers and Dodo Birds 1
2. Life With Blinders Off 7
3. The Tortoise, the Hare & Those Expensive, Time-Consuming Trade Conventions 13
4. What Happens in Vegas 17
5. Communities NEED Repair Shops 19
6. Humble all the way to the bank 25
7. Teaching Employees to Sell: Part One 29
8. Teaching Employees to Sell: Part Two 37
9. Short-Changed Customer Shorts the Till 47
10. What Couldn't be Given Away at $200, Sells like Hotcakes at $2,500! 53
11. My $100,000 Customer 61
12. Your Store: As contagious as a pet rock 67
13. Your Most Important 60 Second Commercial .. 77
14. I Lost a Sale Today 89
15. Your Store: A Stage for a Great Performance .. 95

About the Author 99

Shhhh! It's A Secret

1   Fletchers and Dodo Birds

Our twenty-first century, super-convenient Internet can bring the world to our homes. No one needs to get out of a comfortable chair, drive through obnoxious traffic, find a parking place and, after all that, walk a block and a half to your store just to buy stuff.

Some 'experts' insist, "Brick & mortar retailers are the Dodo birds of business, as extinct as the town fletcher, the arrow maker."

Most Americans' knowledge of bows & arrows is limited to box store toys. Few know the arrow is still being invented, that archery enthusiasts live everywhere. Most big cities have archery specialty stores.

Fifty years ago, a modern fletcher had two choices. He could cater only to local cliental or attempt to sell to a mass merchant such as Sears. If he wanted to sell directly to distant customers, he needed to risk investing in expensive catalogues. Then he had to spend even more money mailing those catalogues to people he hoped were interested.

Today, the net lets any fletcher create an on-line catalogue to sell his wares around the world. Growth is limited by talent, not a fat bankroll.

Some archery dealers have abandoned their stores to the net. Others use the Internet to explain why archery equipment should be personalized and draw people into their stores to a level never before possible.

What does this have to do with your specialty shop?

Everything.

Too often our potential customers aren't even aware of anything beyond box store choices. In the past, it took big money to let people know we independent specialty shops exist, and what we offer that box stores can't. Internet advertising seems almost free.

Just when the Internet made it easier to go against the retail giants, the net also made advertising more dangerous.

You take your time to educate your customer about what choices best fit her exact needs—and believe you will make a big sale, the kind that pays the rent. Your customer is thrilled to finally have his needs met. The anticipated profit is your payment for educating your customer.

Then the customer researches the net, buys the item at cost. An undeserving stranger gets paid for YOUR work!

Should we whine "There's no way to compete with the net!" and just quit?

If we sell _only_ product that people already know about, perhaps we should.

If we sell _only_ product readily available elsewhere, perhaps we should.

If, when teaching about new products, we do nothing to make our store's product different from our competitor's, again, perhaps we should just wave "Good by!" to our customer, abandon him to the net.

What can ANY brick and mortar business offer that the Internet can't?

First, we are time savers.

In many of our ads, I mention, "We research so YOU don't have too." Do you think most people LIKE researching their every purchase? Or would they rather be emailing friends? Playing games? Watching movies?

Secondly, **we are safer**.

Mention the **safety** of "try before you buy." Share horror stories about customers who phoned for help from uncaring, out-of-state, Internet dealers who really do not care.

We, on the other hand, often see our customers at the local grocery store. We MUST care.

Worse, to discourage returns, many Internet dealers make the customer pay for return shipping. What value is a guarantee if the seller knows he will seldom—if ever—have to honor it?

Thirdly, we can customize.

Plus we have another Big Advantage over Internet shops.

Remember the archery stores? Once their customers learn the advantage of trial shooting, they want to touch, feel, smell and—most importantly—try a prospective new piece.

Any demonstration on the net or TV will never be as trusted your customer's own, firsthand, touchy-feely experience.

The final emphasis should always be on your customer's personal, physical experience, something the net can't match.

It is an honest final emphasis because people will like and recommend products only if they feel good using them.

Are our brick and mortar stores the Dodo birds of the business world?

Dodo birds never learned to change their life style when hungry sailors changed their world.

Modern fletchers, unlike Dodo birds, learned and are wealthier than their medieval predecessors.

The choice is up to each of us—to learn or to become a dodo bird.

2   Life With Blinders Off

During the recession of 2008, a friend asked me, "With all that is going wrong with the economy, with all the bad stuff that's happened to you, why don't you quit? There's still a shortage of math teachers."

Have any of your friends asked:

"Isn't it dangerous to own a small business?"

"How can you live, not knowing from one week to the next how much money you will make?'

"Why don't you get a real job?"

Or have bankers ever told you:

"We don't like to loan to small business owners. Their income is too uncertain."

When we first started our small business, loan officers told us our unpredictable income made us a poor loan risks. Before becoming totally self-employed, we had bought and sold three houses. We took debt so seriously we even paid off our student loans years early.

At the same time the bank loan officer was telling us "NO!" our 'secure' employees more easily obtained loans because they had regular, predictable paychecks---paychecks paid by us! Their income was only as 'secure' as our business.

The well-paid banker believed no normal person could, or should, live with our level of economic uncertainty. Many other 'experts' agree.

Have you heard politicians expound:

"People can't function unless they know they will always have a home and a 'reasonable' standard of living."

News commentators talk about, "these times of economic uncertainty" as though economic uncertainty were something new.

For us small business owners across America, the economic uncertainty our neighbors see as terrifying has been daily life from the first moment we decided to be self-employed. Our employed neighbors wonder how we can handle the risks.

When a recession hits, our 'safely employed' neighbors discover, often too late, that their paychecks are only as good as the profitability of their employer. We are like wild horses; the 'safely employed' are harnessed horses. How are we like horses?

Back in the horse and buggy days, one of the greatest dangers came from unexpected side motions. A gust of wind sending leaves swirling could make a horse bolt, putting horse, cart and humans at risk. To prevent panic, buggy drivers put blinders on the horse so he couldn't see anything but a safe road straight ahead.

This prevented unwarranted panic, but it also blinded the horse from real danger.

In the same way, the average employed person has been conned into thinking he is 'safe', the attitude shared by many financial institutions.

The average person is told daily that life should have safety nets for every possible calamity, as though real life can be devoid of danger.

We small business owners are eyes-wide-open buggy drivers; not draft horses wearing blinders.

Jim Collins, author of the international best seller Good to Great, said in his April 2009 Inc article:

*"...My students use to come to me at Stanford and say, 'I'd really like to do something on my own, but I'm just not ready to take that much risk. So I took the job with IBM.' And I would say, 'You're not ready for risk? What's the first thing you learn about investing? Never put all your eggs into one basket. You've just put all your eggs into one basket **that is held by somebody else**"* [emphasis added].

"As an entrepreneur, you know what the risks are. You see them. You understand them. You manage

them. If you join someone else's company, you may not know those risks, and not because they don't exist ...that's a much more exposed position...."

The most common response to Mr. Collin's argument is "But a regular paycheck let's me plan my finances. That feels safer."

His reply?

People confuse predictability with safety and uncertainty with risks.

We business owners must have the ability to face uncertainty; to have faith life will average out. Because we are not relying on just one person to provide our livelihood, we are at less risk than any employee who relies on his boss.

Because we owners are forced to see the big picture, we are not as shocked when disaster strikes.

Our employed neighbors feel more secure only because they are living life with their economic blinders on.

The employee thinks he can see a safe road ahead.

We are the drivers who see the entire road, with all its dangers.

We live with our economic blinders off.

Shhhh! It's A Secret

I became self-employed because anything else is too risky.

3 The Tortoise, the Hare
&
Those Expensive, Time-Consuming Trade Conventions

We've all heard the tale of the tortoise and the hare.

The lowly tortoise challenged the hare to a marathon. The hare agreed. The forest animals gathered to watch the race.

The hare and the tortoise took off. The hare left the tortoise in a cloud of dust. In spite of coughing from all the stirred up dust, the tortoise plodded on towards the distant finish line.

After a long run in the hot sun, the hare decided he needed a little siesta under a shady tree.

Dare he risk the break? The tortoise was a distant speck; the finish line, only a sprint away. Of course he could!

Cool shade, a soft warm breeze, gentle bird song…the hare slept deeply. An hour later, the tortoise plodded past the napping hare.

Another hour passed.

The excited cheers from the watching crowd awoke the hare.

The tortoise was just inches from the finish line.

The hare charged forward, faster than he'd ever run before, only to arrive seconds too late.

The moral Aesop gave was "slow and steady wins the race."

But there is another, more important moral:

The wise race against someone better themselves.

If the hare had raced against another hare, or a road runner, or a cheetah (Now there's motivation!), win or loose he would have run a good race.

Everything we do is a race.

We race to gather money faster than our creditors want it.

We race to accumulate savings faster than we will live.

We race with our competitors, including COSTCO and Wal-Mart, to earn the right to serve our customers.

We race to become a better person.

How good a race we run is as influenced by the quality of our fellow racers as it is by our own ability.

Low ability that continuously pits itself against high ability will astound detractors by eventually doing well.

High ability that decides average is good enough, will remain average. Worse, some high ability people take false pride in achieving average quickly; lazy high-ability will brag about how little effort their accomplishments took and too often mock those who need to work hard.

The person who believes hard work is only for the untalented, risks waking up and, like the hare, discovering the race is lost.

In every field, those at the top agree on one bit of advice: If you want to get better, hang around already successful people.

Every truly successful professional I've met has also shared another life lesson: Until you've helped others learn to succeed, you haven't done anything worthwhile.

What does that have to do with those inconvenient, often expensive, trade conventions?

Want to meet some hares in your line of work? Attend conventions.

Those who can afford to take time out from operating their business to learn more, tend to already be the best in the field. It is a true opportunity to associate with those top performers—to race with hares not tortoises.

When we encounter others on the convention floor, it is also our opportunity to share what we've learned.

No matter what your business specialty, there is bound to be an organization for it.

Don't know of one? Look up your business on the Internet and add 'organizations' to your search.

Can't find one? Check out related blog sites and ask.

Still can't find one?

All organizations started with one person. Perhaps, for your specialty, that person will be you.

How strongly do I believe professional trade shows are worth the time and money? Consider the following article I wrote for *The Floor Care Professional* following a trade convention in Las Vegas.

4 What Happens in Vegas
Inspired by a VDTA Las Vegas Convention

"If you don't read newspapers, you are uninformed. If you do read them, you are misinformed" Mark Twain.

In the spirit of Mark Twain:

"If you don't follow the news, you won't know which business plans to make. If you follow the wrong news, you will be too scared to plan." (me)

Pontificating experts saturate our news with stories that compare American small business to a boxer sinking to the floor from a knock-out punch.

How do those experts think struggling businesses should respond? By waiting for someone else to rescue them! As a keynote speaker said, none of us small business owners are getting a government bail out.

At the convention we got something better: ways to fight back by working **smarter**!

Dealers came from every part of the country.

Both jokes and business plans were shared.

One lady described buying out a competitor's old-time, grime-filled vac shop. She cleaned, painted and updated it; transforming the old vac shop into a popular and profitable Vacuum Store.

During the Friday appreciation time, I talked with several men who successfully used the Internet to drive business into their stores.

Another man told me how (inspired by yours truly) he is now known as a cleaning expert. Women now come to his store to ask advice; and buy recommended problem solvers.

Booths were crammed with a plethora of merchandise.

Vacuum attachments that had looked over-rated in the catalogs were experienced first hand—and ordered.

From the opening awards presentation, to the final minutes Saturday noon, the VDTA show was a celebration of success.

What happened in VDTA/SDTA Vegas—the new demo ideas, the new products, the mutual encouragement—did not stay in Vegas.

We took it home.

5 Communities NEED Repair Shops

Many neighborhoods have that one unpaid person who fixes whatever is broken.

A frequent answer to "How did you start your business?" is, "I was always fixing things for my family and friends just to help out. Then the factory downsized me out of a job. My friends started paying me for fixing things; next thing I knew I was in business! I love it!"

Someone survived a local Big Business downturn by becoming a self-employed repairman, a trivial blip to the community's economy.

Or is it?

When professional city planners try to think of everything a community needs, they seldom consider humble repair shops. Some cities even zone them out of 'nice' retail areas.

City managers have many goals. One of their most important, a key lynch pin to all other goals, is to design communities so as much money as possible will be spent and re-spent locally. Dollars-in-circulation are the economic lifeblood of any community.

Repair shops are powerful dollar-circulating generators.

Consider what happens to two vacuum owners whose vacuums died.

The man who lives in a community without a repair shop will most likely toss his old vacuum. If he buys a new vacuum from a local box store for a $100, about $90 of those dollars leaves his community.

His wallet is left empty.

Life is a challenge.

Now consider a lucky man who took his choked up vacuum to a repair shop, and spent $50 getting it running again. All of that $50 stayed in the community.

On his way home, he stops at a local coffee shop, spends $10.00. About $8.00 will stay in the community.

When he gets home, his wife says, "Let's go to the farmer's market!" They buy some locally grown produce. All that money stays in the community.

On their way home, they pick up milk. That evening, he still has enough change in his pocket to be lunch money for his son.

Because he had a repair shop to go to, over $90 stayed in his community, his kid had milk for his morning cereal and money for lunch. His wife is happy. Life is good.

A few of the many repair specialties include: lawn mower servicing, carpenters, shoe repair (Yes, still exists!), clothing alterations, chainsaw repair, window screen replacements, furniture repair, washing machine repair, air conditioner/ furnace maintenance…

Few enter a repair business because of the glamour of working with broken appliances. Or go into alternations & mending because it is 'Fun Sewing'. Or because they enjoy servicing grimy chainsaws. The multitudes of you-messed it-up so I'll-fix-it-up businesses require skilled diligence. Most lack glamour.

Unglamorous repair professionals often experience a level of control over their personal lives unavailable to most. Many repair businesses are conducive to home-businesses. The self-employed who work from home can be present whenever their children are home. The presence of responsible adults is closely correlated with reduced juvenile crime. A lower crime rate is another valuable contribution to the entire community.

Home business owners have a delightfully short commute to work.

When building improvements are needed, they don't need to choose between putting a fresh coat of paint on their business or their house. All improvements help both places because it is the same place! Better maintained structures add to the total value of the community.

Home based repair businesses can be an excellent life.

Why isn't it more common?

When school teachers ask their students to write the "Want I want to be When I Grow Up" essay, few write "I want to fix things other people rip, wear out or break." in those school assignments. Most students hope to someday provide an honest living for their families; ideally doing something glamorous where they get to wear nice clothes and talk importantly to other people. Or perhaps something exciting, even dangerous. But fix things? Repair is an almost invisible career choice.

Unglamorous fix-it businesses help everyone else afford a little more luxury. Can anyone make a good living for themselves in such humble professions?

According to the book <u>The Millionaire Next Door</u> by Misters Stanley and Danko, in our modern world unglamorous professions are a popular route to glamorous bank accounts.

In tightly zoned communities, homes in areas zoned to allow home based business are usually 50% to 200% <u>more</u> expensive than similar homes in a strictly residential zone.

6   Humble All the Way to the Bank

Is the possibility of wealth through "undesirable labor" only a temporary, modern phenomenon, or is it an enduring economic truth?
Consider the following ancient example from Genesis:

Joseph, a foreign slave in Egypt, became Pharaoh's right hand man by predicting seven years of plentiful harvest to be followed by seven years of severe drought and famine.

Being forewarned, Pharaoh ordered Joseph to store more than enough grain to last during the lean years. When the predicted famine hit, Pharaoh sold the stored grain to both his subjects and starving neighboring peoples. Every year of the famine, the price went up, making Pharaoh much wealthier than before. Joseph became almost as powerful as Pharaoh.

The drought drove Joseph's distant family to send his brothers to Egypt to attempt to buy food. When Joseph recognized his brothers among the thousands who came pleading for grain, he told his brothers if they returned with his father and their families, he would give them all they needed.

When Joseph's brothers returned to Egypt, it wasn't just his twelve brothers and father; it was the whole tribe; their wives, many children, servants, huge flocks and herds. It would have seemed like a small invasion.

Native born Egyptians were so desperate for food they were selling themselves into slavery to feed their families.

Watching so many strangers and animals given the best, would have bred resentment. Even 'divine' pharaohs were known to meet untimely deaths when they became too unpopular.

Joseph wisely forestalled such resentment before it started.

…When Pharaoh shall say…What is your occupation? That ye shall say …cattle…for every shepherd is an abomination unto the Egyptians.*

How could lowly shepherds be worth an Egyptian's notice? How fortunate Joseph's family could take over a necessary but disdainful occupation, freeing the Egyptians from dirtying their hands.

His family's herds and wealth grew.

There can be great profit in activities others consider beneath them.

Shhhh! It's A Secret

* Genesis 46:33-34
This chapter is an abridgement of Lesson 26 from the author's book <u>Live Abundantly! 50 Business Lessons from the Bible.</u>

7   Teaching Employees to Sell: Part One
Showing Love

"*Love your customers and the money will follow.*" Bob Negen

"*No one will care how much you know, until they know how much you care.*" Zig Ziegler

Customers are going to decide if they **want** to buy from you in the first minute. How, in less than sixty seconds, can we show a customer we love and care about them?

More accurately, how can we get our customers to become instantly infatuated with us?

Let's go to the "Instant Love" experts: Hollywood.

Instant infatuation is Love: Hollywood-style.

Remember all those 'first attraction' movie scenes? Most are pretty much the same.

The hero looks at the beautiful lady; the lady returns his look. They stare intently at each other…the longer their eyes lock, the deeper the attraction.

Movie makers know real caring is expressed with direct eye contact, followed by silent reaction BEFORE anything is said…unless the hero is a Jerry Lewis style

Love-Klutz. The klutzes start talking (or stammering & yammering) **immediately**.

Selling Klutzes also yammer immediately. That split-second of silence makes them nervous. They 'know' they can't accomplish anything while standing silent.

How wrong!

Much happens when people are silent, all of it important.

Great actors know their reaction to others is as important—often MORE important—than their own lines. Doubt that? Rent some of the early Schwarzenegger films. He could barely speak English, but could he stare and react!

Lots of forgotten actors had bodies and ambition as great as Schwarzenegger's, but few mastered his silent stares.

As sales people, we must practice silent looks, only with a smile!

First, notice your customer's body language.

Match it!

People feel most at ease with someone like themselves, and matching body language will say "We are soul mates."—even if you are different genders, cultures or racial groups. (Clinical research psychology should be part of every salesman's reading.)

When your customer describes his situation, don't rush to say, "I know just what you need!" Especially if you believe you do.

Instead, pause. (Think early Schwarzenegger, he ALWAYS paused before saying anything important.) Look directly into your customer's eyes; give a slight yes nod.

How long a pause? In proportion to the importance of the request.

Low ticket item, <u>very</u> briefly, then solve the immediate problem.

After that if you wish to introduce a higher ticket item, again look her in the eye, longer pause because you are thinking of something important JUST For HER.

At this point, clerks will TELL the customer about something else to buy.

Just telling someone, "You also need this cool thing I am selling." is giving unsolicited advice.

We have all received unasked for advice from our parents, teachers and significant others.

Do you like being told what to do?

Are our customers any different?

Isn't unasked for advice sometimes called nagging?

Crash and burn infomercials may get away with it, but when dealing with customers one to one, "buy this now" is harsh.

Customers who feel bludgeoned into buying more do not want to return. It is imperative our customers know we love them.

If we shouldn't force-tell our customers about another item, what can we do?

For the last few thousand years, mothers have been telling their daughters "If you want a man to 'discover' he is interested in you, ask him about himself."

Ask a question related to something the customer just purchased.

Example: She just bought thread or fabric. You can ask, "Is this for a special project?" This transforms routine thread-buying from clerk collecting money to caring person interested in her.

This gives you a chance to say something like, "Our other clients with similar projects have learned ------ helped them achieve great results. Would you like to learn more?" This way you are sharing, not pushing, new information. More important, you are using a third party, not you, as a reason to learn more about you sell.

If you sell supplies for equipment that should be serviced regularly, you are probably very aware of people who delay service until what would have been a small problem becomes a too-expensive-to-repair disaster. Most sales ads aimed at getting people to spend money and time on preventative routine maintenance come across as evil nagging. Even our personalized impassioned pleas can have the emotional effect of being told to eat our vegetables.

Casual sales give you the perfect opportunity to lovingly sell the importance of routine maintenance.

From the purchase, you suspect your customer owns a (sewing machine, chainsaw, vacuum cleaner, lawn mower, furnace, pump…).

Ask "How long have you had your (----)?"

The customer answers.

If the item is fairly new, remind your customer when it should have routine maintenance.

If it is old enough it should have been services at least once, ask "When is the last time you had it serviced?"

If too long ago, simply stop smiling, engage deliberate direct eye contact, be worried, pause, say "Oh." Then say nothing.

Only if you are silent long enough can the customer realize you are concerned and then **ask you** why you are worried.

Your direct eye contact tells your customer your care.

Your silence gives her a chance to respond, to feel in control.

Most important, your silence keeps you from being a pushy, nagging salesperson.

An open-ended silence also lets you easily segue into either selling a maintenance service or a new item.

The more expensive the item or service the customer asks about, the longer the pause should be. She is pondering spending a considerable amount of money.

She deserves consideration from you.

Nothing says consideration like being polite.

It is polite to let the other person talk first.

It is respectful to be attentive when spoken to. If you repeat back to her what she said, she knows you were attentive.

Example:

In response to your questions, your customer has just told you his never-been-serviced computer is four years old.

Instead of declaring, "You are overdue for a professional cleaning! Or better yet, a modern replacement!" as though the customer were a wayward child and you the demanding parent.

Try giving neutral, third party information, "We sell several brads of computers. Every manufacturer recommends annual deep dust removal to reduce overheating problems."

Then silently wait for a response.

Most customers will ask either for more information about maintenance service, or indicate they are thinking of buying new. Both ways, you are now in a position to help both your customer and your bank account.

You now have the beginning of a beautiful friendship. But what about telling her you are an expert?

Proverbs 18:28 *Even a fool, when he holdeth his peace, is counted wise: And he that shutteth his lips is esteemed a man of understanding.*

The same thoughtful silence that lets your customer feel in control also makes you look like an expert.

Now it is up to you to be the expert she expects and deserves.

8   Teaching Employees to Sell: Part Two
Sharing Love

Life was once simple. You were self-employed.

If a customer bought from you, you ate.

If he didn't buy from you, you didn't eat.

As you learned to sell, your customers spent more money. Your business grew. Now it is no longer possible for you to do everything.

A lone self-employed person is a job-owner, not a business owner. The moment you become an employer, you join the ranks of business owners. Most new micro-small business owners hire someone else to do the 'safe jobs,' that don't directly affect income, such as routine physical labor or the basic bookkeeping.

Your most important, greatest income producing job is selling the services and/or products you offer. It makes not a bit of difference how good you are if no one knows about you and why your skill is valuable. If you have a typical micro-small business, you must rely on one-to-one selling of your business more than any mass advertising.

You don't dare entrust personal selling to anyone…or do you?

Wouldn't it be nice to be on vacation, and know you are not missing income opportunities?

It is easy to teach someone to work a till, stock shelves and keep your retail space dusted.

Side note: Any micro-small business employee who won't help with routine cleaning should be fired. Immediately. Other employees forced to repeatedly clean up after an in-house slob, soon resent the slob. Resentment creates bad attitudes. Bad attitudes create unhappy customers. Unhappy customers create down right miserable bank accounts.

It is not easy to teach a neophyte to take a customer from willing-to-settle-for-*cheap* to recognizing the greater value of a high end purchase.

Can we shorten the training process?

You and I know that each customer who comes through your door is precious.

People who have always worked for others are often deluded into thinking it doesn't matter how much the customer spends. Good day, bad day, they eat the same.

Ask you employees, "Who is the most valuable person in the store? Who gives you your paycheck?"

The only correct answer: "The customer!"

The first, and most important, lesson to teach?

Each customer is a precious diamond in the rough.

Shhhh! It's A Secret

When diamonds first come out of the ground, they don't look or feel like diamonds. They need to be cleaned and cut to become the sparkling gems on display within the lighted jeweler's case. Any misstep from the stone's first discovery to the finished mounting can result in a valuable gem becoming worthless.

Customers are the same.

The customer always deserves our best—our best appearance, speech, manners and knowledge.

Even Wal-Mart trains people to be clerks.

Selling is much more than clerking; it takes an apprenticeship period to learn it.

To the customer, your selling apprentice will look like a clerk. The clerk/apprentice must be trained on the physical basics of what you sell before he starts clerking. If absolutely no one else is available, he can do an educational presentation to the customer. At all other times the apprentice <u>must</u> request help.

Getting help is not shouting "Hey, Bob, a guy's here to buy a vacuum!"

That kind of request can cost you a sale.

Instead, teach your apprentice to confide to the customer, "I'm just learning about this too. Let me get an expert to help **us**." Then quickly get the best salesperson available.

When the apprentice returns with your expert, he/she should have a well-rehearsed ten second introduction sharing how wonderful your expert is. "This is—, he has thirty years of experience." Or whatever the expert's best-sounding attribute is.

At this point, your beginner can give a brief summation of all he has learned about the customer's needs/wants. Then the apprentice should pause, let your expert salesperson greet the customer.

Where and how the apprentice stands is of vital importance.

If he stands next to your expert salesperson, they will be identified together. Your customer will perceive it as two salespeople against him.

Warning: The next sentence contains information some claim is no longer true. If your customer is a woman, and your employees are both men, two men standing in front of her can be perceived as confrontational. Anything even hinting as confrontational will trigger instinctive wariness and put a negative cloud over her memory. As a woman, I believe this is true, but that may be strictly cultural.

As soon as your apprentice has finished giving The Very Positive Introduction, he should step away from your master salesperson, and next to the customer. Physically and emotionally your customer and your apprentice are now on the same side. Your customer will feel safer.

Side benefit to you: Your apprentice can better watch and learn how it is done!

Your apprentice must notice the customer's posture. Are hands in front, back, or in pockets? How are his/her feet positioned? If your apprentice assumes the same posture as the customer, it will reinforce your customer's identification with him.

Your apprentice is now a selling aid.

First, he is a **mood setter**.

Have you ever watched a comedy in a crowed theater? Notice how if one person smiles at a mildly humorous scene, than another will chuckle; soon the whole crowd is laughing? We humans pick up on the mood of the people around us.

It is now your apprentice's job to listen, to believe every word you speak is *fascinating*. His conversation with the customer should be minimal, ideally no more than a thoughtful nod, or a brief answer to a direct question, then again giving rapt attention to your master salesperson.

The only reason your sales-trainee should leave the presentation is to answer a phone or help another customer; if called away, the apprentice should return as soon as practical.

Learning to be a great salesperson is more important than stocking shelves, cleaning or doing paperwork.

If your store gives any commission credit, it can be a good idea to pay a partial commission to a cooperative apprentice. That can help prevent people trying to swim when they should still be wearing water wings—in other words, a few extra learning dollars can prevent loosing big ticket sales.

After the customer has left, it is tempting to immediately discuss the educational presentation—the sale.

Do not discuss the sale first.

Your first question after the customer leaves should be, "What did you like best about our customer?"

Why?

The first lesson, the customer is precious, must be continuously reinforced.

Too often our society teaches us to look for the negative. If we focus on the negative in anyone, we see them as less valuable and less likeable. The more your employee likes and values his customers, the better he will be able to relate to them.

We **NEED** each and every employee to look for the positive in each and every customer who walks through the door.

What we are asked about, we will look for.

This will teach your employee to look for the nicest, most likeable characteristics in each customer.

He will learn to see each one as a valuable, precious human being; and the rare you-know-what as the aberrations they are.

Looking for the customer's most likeable qualities will help him to see the customer as precious more than customer-as-income lectures ever will.

We all want our friends to have good things.

If what you are selling is a benefit to your customers, and your employees learn to value and like your customers, they will want each customer to have all the benefits your business can offer them.

It's the loving thing to do.

This team-selling apprenticeship period is more than teaching product knowledge—that can be learned reading or watching a video—it is teaching attitude and physical nuance.

What is the best benefit to having the apprentice stand next to the customer?

We who give similar sales pitches several times a day, many days in a row, can get stale. Whoever is the 'master salesperson', especially if it is you, needs to **ask the trainee, "Were you confused?"**

Be aware new employees are frequently afraid of being critical of the boss. It sometimes helps to imply you made some mistakes. You need an honest critique of your performance. Make it safe for your employee to be honest.

Telling an employee you are fallible has the advantage of being true.

Why is it a benefit for you to have a neophyte critique **you**?

It is physically impossible to both do and to watch the doing at the same time. That is why professional performers, from opera singers to football players, have coaches. If you can afford a professional coach to watch your live sales performances, you need to write a book about how you got so rich (unless your first sentence is "First, get a rich uncle."). Our employees are the next best thing, but only if they can fully put themselves into the role of the customer!

From experience, be prepared for humility.

Why should our second question (after asking what they found likeable about the customer) be what did the apprentice find confusing?

People hate confusion.

Confusion kills more sales than high prices ever will.

We who know our message inside and out have difficulty understanding which bits of knowledge we have that are not common knowledge.

We too easily assume too much is understood.

Even if our apprentice never becomes a salesperson, never underestimate his value telling you when you are giving an incomplete message.

9   Short-Changed Customer Shorts the Till

A true story:

"Hi, I'd like to buy a (Brand X vacuum)."

A sparkling new (Brand X) set on my floor. "Here's one. Is this the model you were thinking of?"

"Yes. I've got lots of thick carpet, allergies and pets. My neighbor said this is the best."

From experience, I knew the model she was looking at was a terrible choice for anyone with thick carpet and pets. I described its negative features.

She crinkled her nose in disgust. "Yuck. What would you recommend?"

Confident she recognized my expertise, I went straight to the demo floor, showed her a model I liked and told her how it better fit her needs. She pushed it across the floor. She liked it how gobbled up the fake fur (kapok).

"This seems perfect. How much did you say it was?"

I repeated the price.

"That's a hundred less than I planned to spend! I'll take it."

Minutes later I was carrying her new vacuum out to her car, wishing all sales could be that easy.

The next day, she was back with another lady. Both women glowered at me as though I were on America's most wanted. "You sold me a no good vacuum. I want my money back."

"What's the problem?"

"After vacuuming, my neighbor," She nodded at the woman with her. "Brought over her (Brand X vacuum), and picked up more dirt. You said any problems, I could bring it back. I have a problem with <u>you</u>. You lied. Here's your machine, I want my money."

I was hurt...The cash register quivered in anticipated pain.

"Uh, what happened when you vacuumed again with your new vacuum?"

The buyer looked confused, then thoughtful.

Her neighbor glared. "We didn't bother!"

The buyer regained her tough stance. "Right!"

Another salesperson watched me flounder under their double-header attack. He approached slowly.

"Hi, I see this didn't do an adequate job for you." as though in total agreement.

The friend interrupted. "She doesn't need another sales pitch; just give her money back!"

My fellow salesman looked first at her, then the buyer as he replied, "We just want you to get the vacuum that best suits both your cleaning needs <u>and</u> your budget. Can you tell me a little about the carpet it was used on?"

He gets a detailed description. He looks thoughtful. Silence, then, "Many people with your carpet type are satisfied with one of these." He walks over to the same vacuum she had first wanted and picks it up.

He paused. "Do you also have pet hair or does any one in your family have long hair?"

"Yes! My daughters, cats and dogs all shed."

"Oh." He looked worried, said nothing.

She breaks the silence. "Is that a problem?"

"For this machine, yes. Would you like to see why? It will only take a minute."

Carrying the brand X vacuum, he walks over to the demo floor. The ladies follow.

He shows them the brush roll, explains how it is made. He picks up a similar, worn-out brush roll, shows what dirt and hair did to it. He has them feel the brushes on both the new and worn out Brand X brush roll.

He then hands them a metal brush roll, explains the construction, discusses the advantages to replaceable strips.

Salt is poured onto the floor. Using a manual carpet sweeper, he shows how brush action without suction can clean.

Then he pulls out our favorite brand. Another salt line is poured onto the floor; a quarter is placed beyond the salt.

"You saw how cleaning can be done with no suction. This vacuum" He picks up a step-down from the model my customer bought. "Has a smaller motor than yours. Let's compare carpet cleaning."

He vacuums a third of the salt line with the Brand X, admires the 'excellent' performance. He vacuums up to the quarter, and back. The quarter sits there.

He vacuums a third of the salt line with the step-down vacuum. It vibrates towards the vacuum. He goes up to the quarter. It jiggles into the vacuum.

He **SHOWED** what I only told.

My customer says thank you for the information, but she wants to look around, give it more thought.

I knew this time she and her friend will be checking other brands for the features they both now understand are needed.

I 'cheerfully' refunded my customer's money. My cash register sobbed.

If instead of a rushed, mostly-talking demonstration, I had let her hold both brush rolls; encouraged her to vacuum with both the Brand X and my recommendation; had her examine the agitator; **if I had not short-changed her**; she would have understood which vacuum best fit her needs.

The decision to buy would have been hers; not the result of some salesperson yammering on.

My customer would have had the ability to show her neighbor the obvious advantages of her new vacuum over the Brand X vacuum. And she would still own it.

Even better, her neighbor may have come in, pre-primed to like us, asking about the cool vacuum.

My short-cut "selling" had cost not just the one sale, but referral sales as well.

Three l-o-n-g weeks later.

My customer came in alone. She asked if she could give our favorite brand a second test drive.

This time she kept it.

Selling is teaching.

All specialty stores have products that differ from mass-merchant ordinary. To the specialist, those differences and their advantages may seem obvious, but to the rest of us, they are not. We need to be taught why your (watches, chainsaw, lawn mower, washing machine, thread, glasses, tires, jeans, diamonds,...) are better Quality. We need to be taught what YOU bring to the table as a merchant and skilled professional.

Few of us got 100% when tested on information a teacher only lectured to us. But information we were shown, especially experiments we did for ourselves, that was understood and remembered much longer.

No matter what we are selling, if our customers are to stay sold, it is important to show more than tell what sets our products apart.

Our words are forgotten, and too often misunderstood.

What is experienced is both better remembered and better understood.

10   What Couldn't be Given Away at $200, Sells like Hotcakes at $2,500!

Abridged from Inc. January 2009 Legacy article, p.120:

Mr. James Benson, solar power pioneer, SpaceDev, Inc. founder, and hybrid motor supplier for the first privately funded manned space flight; died October 2008 at the young age of 63.

Mr. Benson was a man who dreamed of commercial space travel. His financial success developing Compusearch software helped him to indulge that dream.

Compusearch, an excellent product, almost failed. Why?

Because of the most common error of all beginning salespeople: selling too low.

*"...In 1983, he co-founded Compusearch, which produced software...**Benson had no luck {selling his program} until a prospect explained that the $200 software seemed too inexpensive to do what it claimed. 'He raised the price to $2,500, and it started to sell like hotcakes,'...**"*

Before the prospect enlightened him, did Mr. Benson believe no one bought from him because he just wasn't a salesman? That selling is some esoteric skill available to only a lucky few?

Or did Mr. Benson believe others 'out there' with bigger research budgets had better software? His product was just too inferior?

Perhaps Benson believed no one bought because he didn't know enough of the 'right' people?

Since he couldn't sell his software at $200, did he ever offer it at $190?

Compusearch was better than the competition. James Benson knew businesses needed his program. He knew he could explain Compusearch. He could not sell it.

Why?

Mr. Benson made the classic error of underestimating his own value.

Just like thousands of small business owners do every day.

For instance, when we sell a repair to our customer what we are selling is our expertise.

Our customers do not know how to judge an unknown repairman...just like Mr. Benson's first customers did not know how to evaluate his unknown software. Customers instead **trust us to tell them what our value is.**

Shhhh! It's A Secret

If one shop advertises "Full Service, Only $19.95" and another just as boldly advertises "Full service, $49.95", most of us will believe the half-priced service is a half-quality service. The lower priced shop will have less credibility.

The same is even more true when it comes to complex skills—such as computer programming.

In forums dedicated to vacuum dealers, vacuum repair people have discussed how raising repair rates increased both customer confidence and their income.

"Drop the price, loose the sale" is equally true on the sales floor.

Imagine you are a customer, listening to a salesman selling you an appliance that is normally $1400, but is on sale today for "Only $1200."

You are thinking, *It looks awesome. Thanks to his great demonstration, I've learned it has the features I want. But how to afford it? I came in planning to spend $300, now I'm considering spending four times that much...Dare I write a check? Use a credit card? What will my family say?*

As you attempt to sort your thoughts, the salesman keeps yakity-yakking. Finally, he's quiet.

You can think.

The salesman interrupts again. "If you buy today, you can have it for another $200 off, only $999."

You think, *Whoa, I almost paid $1200! It's a good thing I kept my mouth shut, or this fast talker might have over-charged me. My family will ridicule me if I pay too much...I better stick to the three hundred dollar model...perhaps one of theirs, but I'm no longer sure they can be trusted.* You say, "That's a lot of money. I'll have to think about it."

To tell the person you no longer highly value his product would be insulting. You are too nice. Just like Mr. Benson's first few dozen prospects didn't wish to offend him by saying his software couldn't be any good because it was too cheap.

Knowing human nature, I can guarantee at least a few who didn't buy the "too cheap" software, said, "James, I would love to give Compusearch a try, but we just don't have an extra $200 in our budget this year. Maybe next time."

Mr. Benson would have left, his belief, "*My price is too high.*" *Intact.*

If you know what you are offering is more valuable than what the competition offers, back your beliefs with action.

Charge more.

When the customer pauses, don't assume he is thinking, '*That's way too much money.*' Don't crash into his thoughtful silence with a "Today only!" offer.

A better way to handle the customer who needs to think?

First, **never delude yourself into believing you are a mind reader**. Remember Mr. Benson's false assumption of over-priced, while his customers in reality thought the price too low?

Second, **give your customer opportunities to think.**

Every time you present new information, be silent; let your customer digest it.

If after a moment of silence he still looks puzzled, he could be thinking of applications, disagreeing with you or still trying to decipher your (to him) confusing words.

An open-ended question will help reveal your customer's thoughts. Examples:

"Would that make life easier for you?"

"Does that sound fun?"

"When I first heard ----, I had trouble believing it. You, too?" (Neutral because implies he might be smarter than you.)

Try giving your silent customer something physical to do---even if just handling the merchandise or an information sheet. Keep quiet while he is physically engaged.

For instance, when showing a high end vacuum, we say, "The physical fit to you is important. Just like two different people will disagree about which car drives better, people will disagree about which vacuum is the most pleasurable to use. Here, just vacuum awhile, go under furniture, use the tools. Any new questions, just ask."

Then take a step away.

If you're a jeweler, you might hand your client two stones, saying, "Hold them up to the light. Which color do you like best," then silently lean away.

This gives your customer a chance to collect his thoughts. If he is trying it, he is interested. When he is through handling your products, you can discuss what he likes and dislikes about each one.

Since nothing man-made is 100% perfect, allow him to decide which compromises he is willing to make. Too often, we salespeople—made nervous by silence—suggest the compromises we think are the most logical.

None of us is our customer.

Shhhh! It's A Secret

   We should never presume which feature is most desired by someone else, which features he is most willing to 'throw away'.
   If we respond to the customer's comments with defining questions or information, then HE selects and owns any compromises, not us.
   Example: At my store, a common compromise is brand new versus almost new merchandise.
   We ask the customer if he would rather have a brand new vacuum, assembled just for him, or save twenty five dollars buying the floor model. Most floor models (the machines we use for demonstration purposes) have been demonstrated only in our store; most with less than 5 hours run time. Floor models have the manufacture's full warranty.
   New employees are shocked how many people who could "barely afford to eat," suddenly turn their noses up at the discounted floor model, and instead choose to pay the full asking price for their 100% new vacuum.
   The higher-priced vacuum has more value to them—just like the higher priced program had more value to Mr. James Benson's customers.
   Should additional discounts prove necessary, find a way that does not devalue your new merchandise.

Ask, "You will benefit from all the features you've seen, but if you had to do without one, which one would it be? Perhaps, by eliminating what you don't need, we can lower the price."

In other words, the discussion is back to compromises, not to-buy or not-to-buy.

What you must never do is compromise your value, to yourself or to others.

Each person who chooses to pay your full price is someone a too-quickly lowered price could have chased away.

Why chance it?

11 My $100,000 Customer

Most purchases in my small retail store are less than $50.00. We have a few high end vacuums, and a couple of very expensive sewing machines, but few of my customers collect expensive merchandise.

Yet I have several $100,000 customers.

The ladies who tie for this position have been customers of mine for years.

A La Betty Crocker (who was based on a composite of the Betty Crocker Company founders), this will be a composite history of:

My $100,000 customer

Let's call her Alice, because when her friends have any kind of cleaning question, they Go Ask Alice.

I first met Alice when she was a newlywed. She & her husband had $50 in wedding gift money to buy a vacuum & had heard my radio ad "S-t-r-e-tch your vacuum dollar with Clean, Like New Vacuums!" They seemed like any other cash-strapped young couple. We stressed that the used vacuum would have a future higher trade-in value since they bought it from us.

Net profit that day: Less than $5.00.

It turned out that Alice's parents needed a new vacuum. At her recommendation, they came in & bought a new, top of the line, Panasonic.

Her mother's church needed an extra vacuum. They bought one of our used ones, and then noticed we sold cleaning supplies.

The church started using our good smelling bathroom cleaner. The ladies at the church came in to buy the bathroom cleaner for their homes.

One of those ladies mentioned troubles with her new puppy…we sold her an effective live bacterial product. She sang its praises to everyone. All her friends with puddle-prone pets came to our store.

The next few years we sold Alice a better vacuum, at least ten vacuums to church members and a new commercial unit for the sanctuary, plus more cleaning supplies.

Several years after that first visit, Alice & her husband still struggled to make ends meet. She decided to clean houses while her two children were in school. She came to us for help because we "taught her how to clean toilets" and she loves her vacuum.

I advised her how to be more professional by such little things as write out in detail what she would do when housecleaning. If a customer wanted to pay her less, to say "OK, but which one of these items do you want me to leave out?" This hint alone became worth gold to her. It allowed her to honorably spend less time at homes that paid less, and more time in the homes of those willing to pay more.

Since she was now a professional, I allowed her to receive case lot rates for items purchased in smaller quantities. (She simply had no place to store larger quantities.)

Whenever I learned about a new technique or more about the chemistry of cleaning, I shared the knowledge.

In short, I helped her to make the transition from struggling amateur to profitable cleaning professional.

Only four years later she asked me to stop recommending her to new clients. She had more business than she could handle and was going to have to raise her rates—again—to cut down on the number of homes she and her employee (That's right, employee. She was now a successful business woman!) cleaned each week.

All of her clients are very successful people. They have to be to be able to afford her. At her recommendation, most of them have bought vacuums and cleaning supplies from me.

Thank you, Alice!

Now that I'm thinking about it, $100,000 is a conservative estimate for how much that first $50 sale was really worth.

I also made a life-long friend.

If you are thinking, 'That works for the cleaning supply business, but not mine.' you are wrong.

What made Alice special wasn't just typical word-of-mouth. When she became a professional user of my products, people valued her words more than others. Likewise, those customers whose friends know them to be cleaning fanatics have more valuable word-of mouth than their "more casual living" acquaintances.

When I first met Alice, there was not a clue how important she would become to my business.

Everyone who comes into my shop is seen as a future Alice.

Specialty businesses have certain customers who use their services on a more extreme level than most. Whether it's the dedicated hobbyist or a professional end-user, it behooves us to offer special attention to our extreme customers.

Shhhh! It's A Secret

We can tell them first about new products, offer special rates, find ways for them to succeed.

We need to become their treasure trove of information.

If in 1990 someone bought a stock for $50 a share, and in 2010 it was worth $100,000, would you think he was lucky? Or smart? Or both?

We have the opportunity to turn $50 customers into $100,000 customers every day—only luck has nothing to do with it.

12   Your Store: As contagious as a pet rock

All of us strive to get good word-of-mouth advertising.

But the ugly truth is that if you have ninety-nine customers who are enthusiastic about how wonderful you are, and one person who thinks you are the scum of the earth, we all know who is going to do the most talking.

And which one will remember us the longest.

Most people have little reason to talk about vacuums, my store's main product. Social small talk is about movies, weather, politics, sports... Vacuums come up as often —and for the same reason as— dentists. People talk about vacuums and dentists when they have a problem.

Our goal: Have happy customers who will enthusiastically talk about us with many different people!

In Malcolm Gladwell's book <u>The Tipping Point</u>, he discusses how retail success and epidemics are similar. A product, like a contagious disease, can exist in small, unnoticed quantities until suddenly a small change occurs that has a BIG effect. It can happen to anything.

When I was a teenager, it happened to pet rocks. (For you youngsters out there: I am not making this up. Ask your elders about pet rocks.)

It can happen to your store.

Think of your store's popularity as an epidemic you want to get started. According to Gladwell's Law of the Few, there are three types of exceptional people who have an effect out of proportion to their number. Convert any one of these types to a "sticky" message, and they will share the message like a sneezer spreads a cold. Mr. Gladwell proves we need to cultivate: connectors, mavens, and salesmen.

Mr. Gladwell defines connectors as those people who regularly socially interact with disperse social groups. This can be the person with best friends who are in all major economic groups; the person who socializes with people from all political parties; the atheist who associates with the deeply religious---anyone who connects disparate cliques.

Mavens see themselves as experts or connoisseurs. What sets mavens apart from other experts is their eagerness to share their opinion. Mavens are frequently self-appointed experts. The TV series Cheers gave us the famous fictional maven, Cliff.

Shhhh! It's A Secret

Salesmen are just what they sound like: people who once they like you, want everyone to come to your store and use your products. Unlike mavens, salesmen don't care which product people buy from you, as long as they buy from you.

It can be difficult to recognize potential connectors, mavens and salesmen.

For those of us with retail specialty shops, there are two types of customer who fulfill all three roles: The Dedicated Self-Employed Professional and The Extreme Hobbyist.

For my business, the customer who fills all three popularity-generating roles is the Self-Employed Professional Housekeeper.

The professional housekeeper often has clients on a different social standing than she is; she "connects" different groups of people.

Professional housekeepers always seek more efficient ways to achieve the results the best-paying clients demand. Their friends know this, and seek their cleaning advice. Because of this, the professional housekeeper becomes an information specialist, a maven.

If you are a professional housekeeper, Cleaning is Survival. You will be emotional about cleaning equipment. Few ordinary people enthuse about cleaning; most people save their excitement for important things like who won the World Series or the latest American Idol competition.

A dedicated housekeeper will break into a big grin or a glaring grimace when mentioning a vacuum. Body language says more than any sales brochure ever will. Emotional cues separate compelling salespeople from the ordinary. Because dedicated cleaning professionals are emotional about their cleaning tools, they are natural salespeople for equipment they like.

If you have a specialty business, you most likely have a few extreme-needs customers.

The dedicated self-employed professionals who patronize your business will have a larger accumulated affect on the success of your business than how much, where and how you advertise.

Any of your extreme-needs customers can be the few who create your tipping point. There are things you can do to encourage those special customers to help tip your store in greater success.

What we do:

From the beginning, we deliberately sought to transform house-keeping men and ladies into our tipping-point sales force.

We attempt to get them the best possible vacuum for their needs and budget, fix it when necessary, and be super sympathetic to any problems.

We do that much with all our customers. It wasn't enough.

When you were dating the person you wanted to marry, did you treat that person any differently than your other friends?

Of course you did.

We needed to do more if we wanted to encourage each and every Dedicated Professional Housekeeper to be our active connector, maven and sales force.

We discovered following Grandma's advice was the best advice: Tell the truth.

We tell each self-employed professional cleaning person she/he is the most important part of our advertising budget.

When do we reveal this?

The moment we learn she is a professional housekeeper. If a customer is
    Buying bags

Checking in a repair
   Looking for a vacuum

and mentions cleaning homes for a living, we say:

"Did you know you are the most important part of our advertising budget?"

We give her time to react either verbally or nonverbally, then explain,

"I bet your friends ask for your cleaning advice all the time."

We wait for her to nod yes. If she or he goes into a story about people hounding him/her for advice, that person is listened to very attentively! This person is GOLD. Listening shows respect.

Remember the sociologist's version of the Golden Rule: Whatever attitude you give to others is the attitude they give to—and about—you. In other words, you will receive what others see you give.

If we want to be remembered with respect and awe, we must respect our customers and find something special to admire about each one.

Each one of the professional cleaning people who come to my store inspires respect and awe. They are women and men who went out into a world of strangers and created their own employment. How could anyone not respect that?

The respect we give is returned.

Anyone who cannot find a reason to respect his customers, might be in the wrong business.

If when first meeting a new cleaning lady, she sings praises about a product we believe to be worthless, we do not immediately dump negativity on her.

Instead we state a positive truth, "You really care about the quality of work you do."

We wait for her to indicate that she cares a great deal about the quality of her work.

Then we confide, "Which is why your friends value what you have to say more than any advertisement we can buy. The EXTRA money I would have spent on advertising I spend directly with QUALIFIED Professionals such as yourself. Would you like to see how much quality you can get for your dollar here?"

Now is the time we can gently introduce choices other than her old stand by's. For anything contrary to her stated preferences we often say, "I once believed the same thing, but I have learned..."

The customer is intelligent, just without our depth of information and experience.

At all times we try to increase her self-confidence, especially when disagreeing with her.

No one is going to spread the word about us, our store or our vacuums if they harbor doubts about themselves. Or believe we insulted them.

After we solved the first problem that brought them into our store, we've done only half the job of making our store as contagious as a pet rock.

We've developed a messenger, but have given her a one note message and a one note reason to come to our store. It helped, but we need to get her to think of us more often.

We need to make the message "stickier."

Cleaning ladies need to know how to get more work done in less time. Every time a professional can get a $10 service completed in half the expected time, that is like getting a $20/hour raise.

The more profitable a cleaning lady is, the more she will enjoy her work and the longer she will stay in the profession.

It is a lot easier to help the same person grow her business skills than to teach a new person the basics every two years.

Ask your Self-Employed Professionals, "What is your most time-consuming, difficult business task?"

Keep written notes about these problems. This requires perseverance and frequent homework.

Whatever our customers say is their biggest problem, we study to become helpful experts.

There is a fine line between being a braggart know-it-all and a friendly information source. Those times when we've crossed that line have had ugly results.

We've learned to avoid saying, "I know this is best!"

Instead, we say things like, "What my other professional clients have found helpful is..."

We keep a list of new tips. Don't tell your customers, **ask** as though sharing a secret: "Have you heard--" Do this even when customer comes for a casual purchase.

Unexpected tips are valued presents. Your dedicated customers will use those tips to make their own services more valued.

You just helped your customer become a better resource to others; she or he is their 'maven.'

Every time someone asks him, "Which product do you prefer?" your customer becomes your outside salesman.

The more problems you have helped him solve, the "stickier" your store's message becomes.

Every time your client conveys your information to someone who has not yet heard of you, your client is your connector.

Your store has a good chance of becoming as contagious as a pet rock.

13 Your Most Important 60 Second Commercial

Has this ever happened to you?

You are at a social gathering. Another guest asks you The Question: "What do you do for a living?"

You: "I have a specialty --- business."

If your micro-small business primary focus is providing specialty information, do you ever hear: "I thought I would need to hire someone like you, but after spending an evening on the Internet I now know everything important about your specialty."

On hearing that, do you think, *How can I politely tell him he is in danger of learning too late 'A little learning is a dangerous thing' is as true today as it was when Pope wrote those words three centuries ago? I've been studying my field for years, and still learning more.*

Worse, you know this nice person you just met could be another victim of bad Internet advice.

Dare you share such thoughts out loud, or do you just mumble something polite?

If your business sells physical products {such as lawn mowers, chain saws, guitars, hair extensions, shoes, facial creams, art supplies, vacuums, bicycles, heaters, computers,… } and your new acquaintance says, "We just bought a new -----, a model X. It's the best one we ever had." While you think, *one of those pieces of infomercial-*

junk, do you say "Glad you like it. If it gives you trouble, bring it by my shop."

A too common response to the idea there could be future problems: "Not likely. We researched it on the Internet."

The person you just met has owned {lawn mowers, chain saws, guitars, hair extensions, shoes, facial creams, art supplies, vacuums, bicycles, heaters, computers,... } before and used them for years, therefore he feels he is an expert. He 'knows' he has no need of your specialized knowledge or years of professional experience. Unless his new {------} malfunctions, he is no more likely to visit your store than if he had never met you.

Variations of these conversations take place for all specialty business owners.

Stymied by the need for social politeness, you waste a chance to advertise your business. Worse, you may leave the impression you equate amateur level information with professional level expertise and endorse over-advertised, under-engineered products

We micro-small-business owners ARE our businesses. Answering "What do you do for a living?" is a no brainer for employees. For us, it can be economic life and death.

For my business, vacuums, it is even worse than for most specialty businesses. Many people equate "Vac Shop" with old time, grimy fix-it shops. Most view vacuuming as drudgery, a topic ideally relegated to someone, anyone, else.

Your specialty may be more esoteric than a humble vac shop; the need for your expertise, more obvious, but your need to create an income generating impression is as great.

Social networking sounds easy in theory, but the reality is difficult. Doing it right, takes a lot of work.

Done right, it will look effortless.

Step One

Think about what you will say in a variety of circumstances. Write out YOUR script.

When I share this step with fellow small business owners, the most common response is "That will sound contrived. I would rather 'go with the flow' of whatever is going on."

Don't worry about sounding too 'canned.' You will naturally make minor variations in different social situations. The better you know your spiel, the less canned it will sound. Ever watch a live play? What sounds more artificial, well rehearsed lines or an actor stumbling for the next words?

Which leads to the second most common protest: "What if I don't remember exactly what I'm suppose to say?"

Don't worry about being perfect. Your old teachers are not going to grade you. Odds are, yours will be the best self-introduction your new friend has ever heard.

Most business owners are easily persuaded they need a social networking speech. The challenge is what to say.

The most common advice---Stress whatever you believe is most important or most impressive about your business---is bad advice

That was not a typo. Your initial self-introduction should not be what YOU find most important, or what YOU see as your biggest bragging point. Why?

Your self introduction should be sixty seconds or less.

Less is better.

Every aspect of your business is important to you. How do you winnow so much into so few seconds? Too long an answer would be the equivalent of answering "How are you?" with a detailed personal health history. Worse, the parts of your business that are most important from your behind-the-scenes perspective will frequently be irrelevant to your friends and future customers.

Why not, "most impressive?" Don't we want friends and customers to have a high opinion of us?

"Most impressive" is full of landmines.

There is a fine line between sharing we are amazingly accomplished professionals and exhibiting we are braggarts. Strangers will rarely tell us we have crossed that line. The opinion of our significant others is too often more influenced by (ahem) 'other factors' than current reality; their opinion can not be counted on to be a reliable guide.

Side note: Let's be honest. It is also ego deflating to insert a little brag into the conversation, and not impress anyone because no one else is knowledgeable enough of your specialty to know you just bragged.

In a short introduction, limit yourself to easily understood facets of your specialty. **If** people ask more questions, you can then describe something that impresses others in your field---and then casually add, "…as is true of my business." Or other words to the effect you are an example of nationally recognized awesomeness. But that comes **AFTER**, not during, your sixty second self-introduction.

The most important reason to avoid first mentioning your business's most important facet is, if you are a typical micro-business owner, when among new friends & acquaintances, you should be selling yourself more than your business.

Regular advertisements are designed to first sell what you sell.

A social network opportunity sells you first, your skills second.

Most people see business proprietors, even us micro-small owners, as strange, not quite normal humans.

Social networking is our opportunity to come across as totally normal, but very superior at the same time. You must reveal you are wonderful, but humble.

No wonder networking is hard for us!

All that said, there are a few similarities with most of the more successful self introductions I have been fortunate to witness.

1 **A single personal reason you are in business**.

Examples:
> **I've the pleasure** of following my parents and grandparents...
>
> **We were lucky** to get out of the corporate rat race...
>
> **My family** wanted to own a business, and after exhaustive research we discovered...
>
> **I always loved** ----, and wanted to share my love of ----- with others.
>
> **I was fortunate** to have earned the opportunity

Those words in bold are bold for a reason. They let you brag without bragging. Associating your current success with factors beyond you, helps suggest humility.

2 **Add reasons why what you offer is not readily available elsewhere, especially if variations of what you sell are available on the Internet or in box stores.,**

Examples:
> **Too many people learn too late**, hours of Internet research are dangerously inferior to years of professional experience.
>
> **Many companies make lower quality** merchandise specifically for box store and Internet sales because those markets cater to price shoppers, not quality seekers.
>
> **Remember how** vacuums **use to last** for ten to twenty years? Now mass-market manufacturers make sure their vacuums wear out too soon.
>
> **Many people settle for economy** reading glasses, unaware those poor quality glasses can damage their eyes.

3 **Combine with one (at most two) reasons existing clients are thankful your business exists.**
Select both selfish and altruistic reasons for thankfulness.

Two examples:

    1: There are so many people who live away from family members. **It's good to be able to help** both inexperienced young adults and the elderly with simple things like belt changes. **Box stores can't afford to take the time to care**.

    2: Box stores are filling our land fills with stacks of disposable vacuums. **It feels good to be able to offer** people a longer-lasting **quality** product that mega-**big corporations don't** want available.

Similar reasons can be found for every specialty business.

4 **Your business name and where you are located by description**.

Don't worry about exact address or hours. Few people remember numbers; they just need enough information to "get a feel" for where you are. Hopefully your business name is simple to remember; and has such obvious spelling anyone can easily look you up on the Internet,

Examples:

    "We were lucky to find an excellent location in the Shopper's Plaza next to Tom's Pizza."

    "Ever notice John's Vac shop across from the library? That's my shop."

Shhhh! It's A Secret

"Have you noticed the new McDonald's on Sunset Boulevard? We are just a block behind it."

When hearing you specialize in {lawn mowers, chain saws, guitars, hair extensions, hair shoes facial creams, art supplies, vacuums, bicycles, heaters, computers,... }, most people will ask which {lawn mowers, chain saws, guitars, hair extensions, shoes facial creams, art supplies, vacuums, bicycles, heaters, computers,... } is best.

A stock answer all of us can use is:

"Remember when clothing manufactures claimed they had one size fits all clothes? Your needs are just as individualistic as your clothing size. At our store you're not at the mercy of the biggest national advertising budget or the latest fad. Box stores are chained to distant corporate boards. I research latest developments and get personal feedback directly from professionals."

It is not enough to write a sixty second self introduction. You need ten and fifteen second versions.

Shorter prepared speeches are especially valuable for people who appear to have zero interest in your specialty. For those individuals, it is usually best to stress strictly personal, but still business related information.

The following format can be used for any specialty business:

1 Brief personal history statement

2 Followed by a discovery statement

3 Concluding with a positive statement about your customers. Specify a trait the person you are talking to has in common with your best customers. This final part will increase the likelihood the person with whom you are casually conversing will eventually visit your business.

One of my ten to fifteen second, self introductions is:

"To earn money for college, I started selling vacuums while in high school. After graduating, I discovered owning a Vac Shop is an easy way to meet above average people such as yourself."

Short, implies a brag, and meets all three objectives.

Side note: If someone expresses surprise your business is an easy way to meet above average people, point out lazy people shop the easy box store way. It takes people who are more inquisitive than average to discover specialty shops. Only those with higher standards fully appreciate better quality. One of the things I personally love about owning a specialty business is: The majority of my customers are above average people!

Read what you have written out loud.

Experiment with different variations.

Now you are ready to test how much your loved ones, love you. Read the self-descriptions you like best to your family. Ask them which ones make them think, "Wow, I'm glad you exist!"

Get their advice on how to make it better. If you have older children, make creating introductions a family project.

When you have your self-introductions ready, it is time for

STEP TWO

Practice, PRACTICE, **PRACTICE**

How often should you practice?

Rehearse every morning while getting ready for work. Rehearse again every evening before going to bed.

Do it in front of a mirror, up close, watching your facial expressions. Then do it in front a full length mirror, critiquing your total body language.

Practice until the words sound as casual, and as easy, as "Hi, how are you?"

National mega-corporations have mega-bucks to advertise their products and services.

You have you.

Remember:

We micro-small-business owners ARE our businesses. How we answer, "What do you do for a living?" can be economic life and death.

If you practice enough, your words will appear spontaneous.

Most important: When watching yourself while practicing, laugh at yourself. Have fun!

Smiles aid memory.

Laughter feeds brain cells.

You are rehearsing mood as much as you are rehearsing words. When you give your sixty second or less self introduction, you want your body language to scream FRIENDLY, never worried or antagonistic.

You socialize with people to have fun; advertising is a lucky byproduct.

Have fun!

14 I Lost a Sale Today

When we need a sale the most, it is too easy to become our own worst selling handicap. A true story:

A prominent builder's name flashed on my computer screen, along with a large sum of past-due money. For the past ten years he has always paid early, now he is over a month late. Why? Should I call him? Give him one more day?

I made the call. "Hi, how's it going? Is your client thrilled with his new built-in vacuum?" I learned the customer was happy with our vacuum installation, but unhappy with other aspects of his new home. The builder's customer is refusing payment until every problem is rectified.

"Some people are too picky for their own good. How about a partial payment to cover my installer's paycheck?"

He seemed relieved, and promised his wife would drop off a partial payment within the hour.

Next I reviewed accounts payable. Half were past due. I had counted on the builder's check to make them all current, but now... Should I pay a little on each? Pick only the oldest and pay that? Was there an insurance or tax payment due?

An employee knocking on my office door rudely interrupted my decision making.

"Fran, someone's here to buy a vacuum."

A new employee, she will get full credit for any sale we help her with.

I rushed out, greeted the customer, "Hi, how are you."

The customer is friendly, answers all the questions about her vacuuming needs. My brain stays focused on the waiting paper work, not her answers.

Through out the demonstration, I recite features by rote instead of personalized benefits.

"You've given me a lot of information; I'll have to think about it." She leaves.

I start to rush back to my paperwork, but the new employee interrupts me. I'm annoyed.

The new employee, "Wow, that was a great demo; I never knew so much about vacuums."

I suddenly realize my brain never left my office. I had recited facts in a rush to get back to paying bills; I had not taken the time to relate each of those facts to the most important person, the customer.

"That was one of the worst demonstrations I've given in a long time."

New employee, "But you showed how awesome that vacuum is."

Me, "I recited facts. She would have saved time reading a brochure."

Very puzzled new employee, "But I thought we showed people the facts."

"But first we **_Listen_**. Only by listening can we personalize the information. She had a cleaning problem. Her problem drove her to come to a vacuum shop on a beautiful day. Instead of listening to her, showing her how we could help solve <u>her</u> problems, I left my mind in the office, concentrating on <u>my</u> problems."

The employee's confusion grew.

I continued, "When someone walks through our door, our job is to help solve their **real problem**. When you go to a doctor because you think you have a cold, a good doctor doesn't assume you have diagnosed yourself correctly. He asks questions, examines you, attempts to discover what the real problem is.

"A good doctor concentrates on **you,** not his personal problems."

I kept my next thought to myself. From many years experience I felt confident if I had done my job right, the customer would have bought a new vacuum today.

Because my thoughts focused more about paying my bills than on the customer, I was less able to pay my bills.

The Rest of the Story

The next day, the employee came running into my office. "She's back. She's still just looking, but has more questions."

A second chance!

I took a deep breath, praying, "Allow me to help this person."

I closed the office door both physically **and mentally**.

My only thought: "How can I best determine her cleaning desires, best match our products with her needs?"

With a relaxed grin, "Hi, how are you this beautiful morning."

This time, I repeated one of her cleaning problems, in her words, before sharing which vacuum feature met the problem.

A thousand dollars later, she left with her new, top of the line, vacuum.

"Fran, you gave her so much more information yesterday. Today you just repeated her words, and said nothing new. Yet today she bought. Why?"

"Because today I listened to her; made her problems important. I explained every fact in terms of those problems. If I had focused on her yesterday like I did today, she would have bought yesterday."

15 Your Store: A Stage for a Great Performance

When someone enters your store, he enters your theater.

Each employee is a performer; *every* item, a stage prop.

The first thing your customer notices is your store's cleanliness.

I went by the field of the slothful…it was all over grown with weeds….the stone wall …broken down…so shall thy poverty come…(Proverbs 24:30)

A trashed environment implies you are trash. Worse, just like sleazy looking theaters attract sleazier looking patrons, dirty stores attract questionable customers. Clean attracts people who value cleanliness.

Broadway producers know the right wardrobe can make a mediocre performance seem great. Wardrobe also defines your business.

The military, baseball teams, even the girl scouts, have uniforms. Shop uniforms increase a sense of belonging and tell the public "This person is special."

Even without shop uniforms, clothing choice tells the world how you want to be seen. Customers feel more at ease if they perceive you as being like themselves.

One of the easiest ways to do this is to dress like the people with whom you *most* want to do business. Politicians know this. That's why they wear cowboy hats in Texas and baseball caps in Minnesota.

You have a spotless, attractive business. You and your staff are dressed for success, but people don't buy from well-dressed mannequins.

Your most important need? A script!

It can be broad, general directions (like the so-called impromptu performances), or a detailed script.

You must know what it is you want the public to learn about your products, and share that knowledge with your employees. Just like a Broadway Theater rehearses, each of you must practice, Practice, **PRACTICE** your lines. Whenever there is a lull in business, even while stocking shelves, ask your employees (and yourself) questions a customer might ask.

Someone watching a Broadway play doesn't care if the leading lady has a headache or the villain a cold. He just wants entertainment. He'll tell everyone if the show was exceptionally bad or good. Mediocre is forgotten.

Likewise, if your customer leaves your shop feeling entertained (and better-than-infomercial educated), he **will** talk about you.

Bad experiences are also relived.

Blah, ho-hum shopping is forgotten even faster than boring shows.

Like a curtain rises on Broadway, the front door to your shop opens…

Smile!

This above chapter is a modified abridgement of lesson 36 from *Live Abundantly! 50 Business Lessons from the Bible* by F. E. Tabor, available from Amazon and Kindle

About the Author

From second grade to beginning college, Fran dreamed of becoming a scientist. While going to college, she sold vacuums door to door to help pay for her education.

After graduating, she planned to become a teacher, but instead, she and her husband bought a small building used to repair trucks. One truck bay housed their fledgling business; the other, their living quarters. They had enough cash to last three months, if they gave up eating.

Fran enjoyed learning more about the vacuum cleaner industry; it became her new scientific research.

She enjoyed sharing what she learned. Fran discovered selling is teaching.

In only six years they doubled the building size, bought a separate home and had two beautiful daughters.

Today that small, 600 square foot vacuum shop has grown to a 9,000 square foot building and those daughters are now parents.

Fran's other books:

Live Abundantly!
50 Business Lessons from the Bible

Can the Bible that guided primitive goat herders be relevant to 21st century Mega Corporations, and small 'Mom & Pop' shops? YES!

The fifty short lessons in *Live Abundantly!* will help you re-discover why the world's most practical business guide is the Holy Bible.

When not thinking business, Fran enjoys writing stories. Her fiction includes:

Eagle Rock.
A romantic murder mystery

A big city girl inherits her brother's buffalo ranch, and learns almost too late his death was not an accident.

To Own Two Suns
An epic first contact novel

Unknown to earth, two feuding alien clans vie for the right to colonize earth. First the two clans must exterminate the pathetically primitive humans, then they will fight each other for sole ownership of our solar system. A research vessel sent from earth to explore the Kuiper belt beyond Pluto unexpectedly encounters a lone scout from the weaker clan. Against seemingly insurmountable cultural barriers, a fragile human-alien friendship forms. Can the improbable friendship prevent humanity's extermination?

Amazon, Kindle and most online bookstores carry Fran's books under the name F. E. Tabor.

www.ingramcontent.com/pod-product-compliance
Lightning Source LLC
Chambersburg PA
CBHW082251220526
45469CB00009B/2953